Fortran Crash Course

By: PG WIZARD BOOKS

Step By Step Guide To Mastering Fortran Programming!

Fortran Crash Course: Step By Step Guide To Mastering Fortran Programming!

Table of Contents

Introduction

Many beginners to coding worry that they are not going to be able to learn how to work with a new coding language. They feel that it is going to be too difficult to learn the language and that they will either not be able to do some of the programming that they want or that they just won't understand what is being said in the information. But when it comes to working with Fortran, you will find that learning how to code is a simple process.

In this guidebook, we are going to start out by talking about some of the information that comes with Fortran. We will also work on the first code for this language and discuss all the different parts that are going to be found inside of your code. This is a simple introduction to help you get some practice with writing your own code and ensures that you are able to get into some of the more complex situations that we will discuss later on.

Once we have these basics down, we are going to move on to some of the other things that you are able to do when it comes to working on your code in Fortran. We will take a look at writing some of your own loop statements, what strings and arrays are, working with conditional statements, and so much more. Even as a beginner, you will be able to use these options in order to make a really strong code and program as you want it.

When you are ready to get into coding and want to make sure that you are designing something that is strong and will work the way that you want, Fortran is one of the best coding languages to help you learn how to get it done. Make sure to use this guidebook to help you to get the basics to work with Fortran for all your coding needs.

Chapter 1: Learning the Basics of Fortran

As a beginner, you may have times that you are worried that a new coding language will be too hard for you to learn. You want to make your own programs, learn how to work in different operating systems, or have another goal that you would like to accomplish, but you worry that it is going to be too much work for you to accomplish because it will be too hard to do. But when it comes to learning how to work with Fortran (which is basically a contraction of Formula Translation), you are working with a great language that is designed for beginners, even for those that have no experience in coding before.

Fortran is considered one of the oldest programming languages that you can use and this can be a benefit as well as an issue. It is beneficial because you will be able to find this language anywhere that you want to look and the compiler, as well as the other add-ons, are all going to be free. It is a coding language that many scientists and engineers like to use because of all the functions that are built in and the fact that it is easily used with mathematical constructs. There are also many other things that you are able to do with this coding language, and since it is one of the oldest options around, you are sure to find lots of help and answers to ensure that you get the project done right.

What will I need to get started?

When you are ready to get started with Fortran, you will need to bring out a new text editor. There are several of these that are available, and you can choose the one that works for you. You need this because it allows you to out the codes so that the compiler, which you will need next, will be able to read out what you are doing and tell the computer how to behave. You are not able to use a word processor for this because these kinds of applications are not going to save files in plain text, which is required to make the compiler do its job.

Next on the list is the compiler. There are many options out there and most of them are going to be free as well so you can download these and not have to worry about adding in costs. Basically the compiler is going to take the words that you have written in the text editor and then change them around into something that the computer is actually able to read. You will just need to save your code and then the compiler will be able to execute it.

Some people find that working with an Integrated Development Environment, or IDE, is a great way to help make this a lot easier. This IDE is going to work similar to the text editor and the compiler in one so it saves you some time, especially when it comes to troubleshooting the written code. For those who are working on Windows computers, the IDE is really a good idea because it has an interface that is easy to sue and similar to what you are used to seeing on the Windows computer.

As mentioned, you could just use the text editor and the compiler, but the IDE does make it a bit easier to write your code. These combine both of the other two products in one and it is able to understand syntaxes of the code easily. In fact, it is going to be able to catch some of the errors that come up in the code as you are typing, saving a lot of time and accidents in the process.

The benefits of using Fortran for your coding

There are so many reasons why you may want to consider using Fortran as your coding language of choice. Whether you are looking to use it on the side as another coding language to master or this is one of the first coding languages that you are going to work with, the benefits of choosing this one are amazing. Some of the reasons that you would want to work with the Fortran coding language include:

- Easy to use: Fortran was designed for the beginner to learn how to use it. It is a simple language to work with and after looking at some of the codes in this book, you are sure to see that it is easy enough to learn how to work with.
- Has been around for a long time: Fortran is one of the first coding languages that came available for coders to use in their homes. This is a good thing because it is simplistic and easy to use. We are going to work on a few different codes inside of this guidebook and you will find that most of them are pretty straight forward and easy to write, even if you are a beginner. While some people feel that the fact that Fortran has been around for so long is a bad thing, it can mean so

many good things for helping you to get the very best when working in coding.

- Great for the scientific community: this is a language that anyone is able to use for their own needs, but it is specifically important when it comes to the scientific community. If you have an occupation that is in this field, you will find that it is a good idea to learn how to use the Fortran code.

- Lots of programs still use it: even though this is an older coding language that you can use, there are still a lot of programs that use it. This means that you will have plenty of chances to use this programming language and to get some more practice.

- Can be modified for other languages: Fortran is one of the earliest coding languages that is out there so it has had many adaptations over the years. This means that there are versions that you are able to use and combine with some of your other programming languages. This makes it easier to do some of the more powerful things that you want to do with your coding.

- It is free: all the stuff that you need for Fortran, from the software itself to the IDE that you want to use with it, is all free to use. This makes it easier for everyone to use this language because you won't have to worry about all the costs that are associated with it.

- Has a big community: when it comes to using a brand new language, you want to make sure that you have a community that is able to answer your questions and make sure that you going on the right track. Since Fortran has been around for so long, there are many people who know how to use this and can be there to help you out.

There are many benefits to using the Fortran coding language. While some people prefer to go with another option that is easier or newer to use, there are still many people who want to work with Fortran because it is one of the first. It is a simplistic language to learn how to use even as a beginner, and it is able to get a lot of the coding and programming done that you would like. If you are looking for a coding language that is pretty easy to work with and is meant for beginners, you won't go wrong when choosing Fortran.

How to test my first code

Now that we have spent some time talking about the things that you need to get started with the Fortran coding, it is time to test out one of our first codes. Once you have taken the time to install the IDE that you would like to use, it is time to double click on the icon so that the programming environment is going to open up. You can then create a brand new file but keep in mind that you may need to select on a Fortran file when you do this, just in case the IDE that you picked is able to read more than one language. So you will need to give it the extension of .f95 rather than of .txt so that you are able to compile these statements a bit later on.

One thing to keep in mind is that there are some other extensions that you are able to use when it comes to Fortran including .FOR, .F, and FPP. These extensions are going to tell the compiler was standards you are following with the work you do so make sure that you pick the one that you want and stick with it. You can experiment a bit to figure out which one you want to use.

So once you are done picking out the extension that you would like to use (we are going to stick with the .f95 one for now), we are going to need to type out the following code to get started:

program mytest

!this is a test

Print *, 'This is an output test'

end program mytest

After we have taken the time to type out this bit of code, it is time to execute it inside of the IDE. Your compiler will then go through and double check the parts of the code, looking to see if you have made any errors in the code before trying to run it. If there are any errors that show up, the IDE will let you know and ask you to fix it. If there aren't any troubles with the code, the compiler is going to generate and then execute the file. Basically, with this one you are going to find that the words "This is an output test" will show up on the screen if you typed it in the right way.

Breaking down this code

Now that we have taken some time to write our own code, it is time to break it down to make a bit more sense. Like a lot of the other coding languages that are out there, the Fortran language is going to take care of the different lines of the code, which are called statements, and then decide what it is going to do with each of them. So in the first line, the program is going to state the name of the program that you are trying to work with.

Then moving on to the second line, you are working with a comment. This basically means that you are writing a little note for yourself or for the other programmers that are taking a look at the code. The compiler knows that it shouldn't execute the comment since this is just a little note. You can add in as many comments as you would like inside of the code to describe what the different parts are going to do.

The third line of the code is the output command that is going to tell the compiler what it is supposed to display on the screen. It is going to show up in a single quote. You can make this statement as long or short as you would like, just make sure that you are using the right options with it. And then in the last line, the statement is terminating, or ending, the program that you just write.

Now, this is a pretty basic option that we are working on and only has four lines. There are many options that you are able to do with Fortran that will use more lines to get it done depending on the things that you are doing inside the code. There are also a few versions of Fortran that will have the code look a bit different. Basically all of them need to have the four same parts including the program name, the output statements (you may have more than one of these in some cases), end of program, and comments if you need them.

Making sure that you have all the right parts in place in order to write the code is important to helping the compiler to work with you on creating the code. And while there are many different data types that you are able to use, as we will discuss as we go on in this guidebook, they can be as simple or as difficult as you need to make the code work.

Chapter 2: Working on Loops in Fortran

When you are working on writing your own code inside of Fortran, you need to understand how to work with loops. There are many different times when you will want the code to keep repeating something, or do a specific action more than once. With the most basic form of your code, you would need to write this part of the code over and over again. Now, if you just want the code to repeat a few times, this may not seem like such a big deal, but what happens when you want to write out the code 100 times? Rewriting the same part 100 times can get tiring and old pretty quickly.

But with loops, you are able to tell the compiler to repeat the same steps until the conditions are no longer true. This could be five times and it could be 1000 times, but you would just need to write out a few lines of code to make this happen. Rather than having to write out the same instructions over and over again, you are able to set up the loop to do the same functions over and over again.

There are several different components that are going to be found inside of a loop to make sure that it is going to work. The main components include:

- Step: this component is going to tell the compiler that the procedure will need to be repeated at least once.
- Start: this is going to tell the compiler that it is at the beginning of your loop.
- Stop: this is going to tell the compiler that it is at the end of your loop.
- Var: this is a variable. It is in charge of telling the compiler how many times that you would need to have your code repeated.

How do these loops work?

Loops are going to begin when you set the start and then you define the var. they will explore what concept you are working with inside the var and decide when the conditions have no longer been met so this will all start. As soon as your statement is executed once, the amount to the var is going to go up by one so that you don't end up in an endless loop. So, if you want to make a table that goes from one to ten, the var would start at one and then each time it goes up by one until it reaches ten. Let's take a look at a sample code that shows how the loop function is going to work:

```fortran
program loop_factorial

implicit none


        !definition of variables

        Integer::xfact=1

        Integer::x


        !computations of factorials

        Do x=1, 15

                Xfact=xfact*1

                Write*, x, xfact

        End do

End program loop_factorial
```

This one is a bit longer than what we are used to with the other code we wrote, but it does show how the loop is going to work for you. This one is going to make sure that the variable will keep going up by one each time that you work with it, helping to keep things organized and to ensure that you don't end up in an endless loop. If you do end up with a loop that doesn't have a stop point, you are going to get stuck inside of the code and have trouble getting out without closing the whole program.

There are a few different types of loops that you are able to work with. Some are going to check the conditions of the statement before determining whether or not to run the loop. If the conditions are not true from the beginning, you are not going to get the loop to run at all and it is going to head on to the next part of the code. This is known as the for loop. And then the do while loop is going to run the loop at least one time, and then run check the options to see if it meets the condition. The choice can be the same, but it does depend on whether you want the code to run one time or it doesn't matter.

The loop is one of the best things that you can work with when trying to make your code look nice and organized when on Fortran. You will be able to tell the loop how many times you would like it to run through the program, just using a few lines rather than rewriting the code all of the time. This is an efficient way to work inside of your code and ensures that the code is still able to work properly.

Chapter 3: Working with Strings and Arrays

When you are working with Fortran, you will find that strings and arrays are great ways to help keep the code organized. There are certain ways that you will be able to work with these in order to get them to execute inside of the code properly. In this chapter, we are going to spend some time talking about what strings and arrays are and how you would be able to work with them inside your code.

What are strings?

Inside of the Fortran code, all characters are going to be seen as one of two elements. They are seen as either single characters or contiguous strings. So what is the difference between them? With a contiguous string, you will notice that their length for syntax declaration is going to be passed, they will allow you to do notations on the substring, they won't allow you to do notation on arrays, they can contain descriptors if needed, and in some cases there are going to be hidden arguments inside.

When you want to declare a string inside of Fortran, you are going to use rules that are similar to declaring some of the other variables. So in order to do this, you would use the following option (we are giving the string an assignment of 10):

specifier :: variable_name

character(len=10)::name

Now in addition to working on the string, you will be able to work on substrings, which are basically just smaller parts of the string. They are going to be any part of the program that is executed and you are able to extract them if you wish. For example, if you have a long string that is several sentences long, you could work on a substring and just take out a few of the words to make it easier to read if you want. Here is an example of how you would be able to take out substrings from the string inside the code:

```
program string_concatenation

implicit non


    character (len=5) :: name

    character (len=50) :: announcement

    character (len=50) :: message


    name = 'Dana Caulfield'

    announcement = 'This is'

    message = 'I would like to give you a warm welcome to Prescott
Academy!'


print *, announcement, name

print * , message

end program string_concatenation
```

With this option you are going to get the message "This is Dana Caulfield. I
would like to give you a warm welcome to Prescott Academy!" You are able
to choose how much of the message you would like to do and you can keep
it all on one line or on more than one. For example, you could choose to
just have "This is Dana Caulfield" show up on the screen if you would like.
This gives you some options to have a longer phrase there if you would like
while also keeping it so that you get smaller patches as well.

Concatenation

Another thing that we are going to take a look at when working inside of
Fortran is known as concatenation. You are going to notice that it will use
the (//) symbol in order to show that this is inside the code. The
concatenation property is the one that describes which programs are able
to link back to each other. Because of these connections that are

established, the main goal is to either draw attention over to another branch in the program, or to make sure that the framework is solid. In some cases the links are going to be for two separate programs, but often the subjects are going to be single elements.

You can also work with a process that is known as trimming. This is when you want to cut out parts of the line that are not necessary so that you get the right result to show up. Since there can often be elements inside the program that aren't needed and are known as trailing blanks, the process of trimming is going to help to get rid of some of this clutter so that you are able to just use the portions that are needed. It also helps your compiler to be able to read through the code faster.

There are a lot of things that you are able to do with the strings inside of your projects and you will be able to mess around with them a bit to get the strings to work out the way that you want. But using concatenation and trimming will help to ensure that you are using the strings in the proper manner.

Arrays

Arrays are another important part of working on your code. They are going to be in charge of storing information, such as variables and characters, that are similar. If the piles of data aren't stored in the proper way, it is going to be really hard for the computer to be able to interpret them. However, when you use the arrays properly to put this information in the right places, the compiler is going to have a better chance at running the program and the functions will be executed in the proper way. Some of the things that you should remember about arrays to make it easier include:

- If you would like to specify the individual elements, you are going to need to address them using the subscripts. The first element is going to have the subscript of 1.
- If you see the term "extent' it is going to describe the elements that are along a dimension. Keep in mind that this is a numerical value.
- On the other hand, if you see the term rank, it is going to describe the dimensions that they have, using a numerical value as well.
- When you see the term "size" this is going to describe the elements that the array has, using numerical values again.
- The shape of the array is going to consist of elements.
- They are going to be declared with the attribute of dimension.

- They are going to be linked to memory locations that are contiguous.

There are two types of arrays that you are able to find inside of the Fortran language. The one-dimensional arrays are the ones that will serve as vectors while the two-dimensional arrays are the ones that will serve as the matrices.

Now that we know a little bit more about arrays, it is time to understand how you are going to be able to declare the arrays. Luckily this is a process that is pretty easy to complete. The rule is to specify the dimension that you desire, and then the compiler will be able to take a look at the elements that are involved and determine if they are an integer or real. For example, if you want to declare an array that is the Caulfield Lair and you want to give it seven elements, you would use the following code to make it happen:

real, dimension (7) :: Caulfield Lair.

Now you can also choose to declare an array that is two dimensional. Let's say that we are still using the example of Caulfield Lair from above, but we are going to make it so that the elements are 7 by 7. To do this, we are going to use the following syntax:

integer, dimension (7, 7) :: Caulfield Lair.

If you would like to make sure that you are assigning the right values to your arrays, you will find that the process is pretty simple. You just need to work on the array and then enter in the amount that you would like to use. You do have some choices when it comes to doing this because you can either do it on a single element that you want to change or you can work it out on the whole array. Let's take a look at an example of how this would work. Let's say that we want to add in the value of 3 to all of the elements would need the following code:

```
do I = 1, 7

    Caulfield Lair = i*3.0
```

16

end program do.

But on the other hand, if you would like to assign the value of 3 to just the
first level of the array and then add different numbers to the other levels,
you would need to use the following code to make it happen:

Caulfield Lair (1) = 3

Working with strings and arrays are a good way to make sure that you are
getting the code to work in the right way. The strings are going to be
statements that happen inside the code and make it easier for you to write
out the different things that you would like to have happen, either by
adding in the whole string to the code or just having a few parts as you see
fit. The arrays are going to be responsible for holding large pieces of data in
a way that is easier to look through and reach inside the code. Both of these
are going to be important to ensuring that you get more out of the code and
that   it   works   the   way   that   you   want.

Chapter 4: Manipulating the Variable Amounts

Now at this point we are going to take some time to look at the different operators and variables that you are able to use inside of your code. So far at this point we have learned a bit about how to create a simple program. But there is a lot of manipulation that you are can do inside the code and operators are a great way to help you to do this. The operators inside of Fortran is going to be a great way to do mathematical functions while also getting these results to show up on the screen. With all that we have learned so far about this program, it is now possible to work on a short program on our own that will help to manipulate the amounts of variables. So basically inside of this chapter, we are going to learn how to make our program in Fortran do some basic math.

First we need to take a look at what the variable is all about. A variable is basically a little container that is going to store information inside of the memory of the computer. You are able to use these to hold either one or more value of your choice, and you are able to assign this either at the beginning of your block of code or when the code is being executed.

Assigning a variable is going to be pretty easy to accomplish. You will just need to use the (=) in order to pick the value that you would like to use along with the variable. You are able to add more than one value to the same variable if you would like to store them together in the code, but for the most part, it is just going to be one variable that you are working with. You can add in many different variables inside of the code, but the operators that we are going to talk about in a minute help to make it easier to get this all done.

Before we get too far into making this kind of program, we are going to take some time to work with operators. While these are pretty simple, there are some times when they can seem confusing and will make you wonder what they mean. The trick with these is to not think of them as mathematical symbols. For example, when it comes to writing out a = 2, you should see this as the value of 2 is going to be stored inside the memory of your computer that is labeled as a. Here is another example that you can use:

a = 2

b = 3

c = a + b

In the statement that we did above, you will see that the value of 2 is going
to be stored as the memory location that is a and then you will see that the
value of 3 is stored in the memory location that is called be. And then when
you add the values of a and b together, you are going to store that result
under the memory location of c. Keep in mind with this one that you are
not able to write out this kind of equation as a + b = c because the compiler
is going to see this as an error. The one variable needs to be on the left-
hand side of your symbol and then you can have as many of the variables as
you would like on the right-hand side, but mixing these around are going to
cause an error message.

Arithmetic operators

Now that we have looked at some examples of operators, it is time to work
with some of the operators that you need. Not all of the math symbols that
you will need are going to show up on the keyboard, but the Fortran does
have some of its own symbols that you are able to use in order to represent
the different math operands that you are able to use. Some of the most
common arithmetic operators that you are able to use on your language
includes:

- (+): this is the one that you are going to use for addition
- (-): this is the one that you are going to use for subtraction in the
  code.
- (*): this is the one that you are going to use for multiplication
- (/): this is the one that you can use for division

One thing to note with these is that you can use more than one of the
symbols, whether you are using three addition signs or an addition and a
division symbol, inside the same part of code. You are able to use as many
of these as you want, but you need to use the order of operands to do it.
This means that you will need to do all of the multiplication, then the
division, addition, and subtraction, going from left to right to make sure
that the compiler is going to give you the right answer.

Other parts of your code

As a beginner, you will wonder what all the blanks, or the skip positions, are inside of the program. Some people choose to write out their programs without using these at all, but for the most part, the programmers like to include these inside of their code in order to make it easier to read. You are able to choose how you would like to use a skip position, but you should include at least a few to make sure that your code is easier to read through.

There are also some special characters that you are able to work with inside of your code. These are used in order to deliver the function that you want. These are going to seem pretty simple and plain but you need to be careful about how you use them. If you use them the wrong way or place two of them into the code right next to each other, you could end up with conditions that cancel each other. Some of the special characters that are found inside of Fortran and that you should watch out for include:

- (/): this one is going to specify another line
- ("): to output strings
- (:): this is going to terminate a list
- () this is going to categorize the descriptors.

Descriptors can be a tool that you are able to use and they are variables that are going to specify the amount of data that is required for a conversion. It is a good idea to keep track of the usage of these since the process may not end unless you add in the right descriptor is placed inside. Some of the descriptors that you can use include:

- A: repetition
- D: this one is for digits next to your decimal points.
- E: this is for an exponential number
- M: this is the minimum amount of digits.
- W: this is width in total characters.

You are going to be able to use all of these different parts to help you to get the code to work the way that you would like. You can mix and match a few of the parts to get the variable to be the right number, to store it in the right place inside the code and to do so much more. When you are able to add in the operators of the Fortran code, work with the blanks or the skip positions to make the code easier to use, and add in the special characters and the descriptors to the code, you are going to get a lot of power and options inside of the code.

Chapter 5: Working with Conditional Statements

At this point, we are going to take some time to look at the if statements. These are the most basic of the conditional statements and you will find that they are pretty straightforward. With this one, you will set the condition that needs to be met as well as the action that will show up at the same time with it. If the user puts in an input that matches, you will see that the program puts up the action that you choose. On the other hand, since this is a simple equation to work with, when the user puts in an input that is seen as false, the program is just going to end because you didn't set up an action.

So for this one, let's say that you just want people who are 18 to be able to get into the website. You would set up the if statement to accept any answer that is 18 and above. If the user places their age inside to be 20, the action (such a statement that you choose) will be executed by the compiler. But if the user puts in that their age is 16, then the program is going to see that this answer is false compared to the conditions that you set, and since you are using the if statement, nothing is going to happen.

Now there are some issues that can come up with this, but let's just focus on learning the syntax and getting this part down. Take a look at the syntax below for this:

if (x == 1) then

print *, 'turn left'

end if

The logical operator is the one that is used in this example along with the statement of if..then..end if. Note the expression that comes after the if statement. It is going to provide you with a test, something that is necessary when you are trying to imply a condition. In this case, we are going to assume that the "x" variable is an integer. One of the values that it can be is equal to 1. Interpreting this as a logical operation, the program is going to test to see if the value of the variable is 1. Then it will check if this is true or not. If your variable is 1, then the statements that come next will be executed which in this case would be the words "turn left". Then the end if is going to terminate the program that you are working on.

The if...else statements

As we mentioned in the last part, the if statement is going to be pretty basic
and there are some issues with it. Your user may very well be 16 years old
and it isn't a good idea to have the program just end if they put in this
answer. You most likely will want to have some message come up at least,
so that the user doesn't assume that something is wrong with the program.
For example, if they put that their age is over 18, you would want to set it
up to say something like "Welcome to the site!" and then have the next
action be that they can get in. But if they put in that they are 16 or
something else, you would rather have a message like "Only those over 18
are allowed in the game!" than having the program just end.

The if...else statement is able to help you to do that. You would set it up like
the first part that we had above, but then you would add the else that
catches anything that is considered false by the compiler based on the
conditions that you set. This allows you to have an answer, any answer,
come up regardless of what input the user is giving to you. This makes it
much more clean cut and easier to deal with and doesn't leave the user
wondering what is wrong with the user.

In addition, you are able to make it so that there are several options that
come up. Let's say that you would like to have someone pick out their
favorite color of either red, green, yellow, or blue. You would just need to
write out more of the else sections of this code would just keep going.
Another really useful thing for you to learn how to use inside of your
Fortran code is the conditional statement. These are really great because
they allow you to have some extra power and choices inside of the code.
These will allow you to put in the conditions that need to be met in order to
get different statements or actions to occur. They can be really simple, such
as the if statement, where you will only have an action happen when the
answer is inputted is true compared to your conditions, you can have it so
that a different action will happen based on if the answer is true or false
based on your condition, or you can give the user some choices.

You can decide what conditions need to be met before you allow the user to
put in their information. This allows the code to keep things simple and it
can look at your conditions before executing what you would like to have
happen. You can make these as complex or as simple as you would like, but
remember that you do need to base these on Boolean expressions. You

have to leave the answer as either true or false based on the conditions that
you set.

Don't worry if this sounds complicated right now. We are going to take
some time to look over the different conditional statements that you are
able to work with and help you to get the results that you want, no matter
what kind of conditional statement you are working with.

The if statements

down the line, taking a look through each condition and statement that you
put onto the screen. You can also add in a catch or break at the end so if the
user picks pink or another color that isn't listed there so they still get an
answer.

There are so many options that you are able to do with the if...else
statements and they can really open up a lot of what you are able to do
inside of your code. You can make them as simple or as complex as you
would like, adding in more sections or just having a true and false option.
Mess around with this a bit and see what you are able to come up with on
your if...else statements.

Conclusion

Working in a coding language can be difficult no matter who you are. Many beginners are worried that they are not going to be able to find the answers to getting started or that it is just going to be too hard for them to pick out how to work with this code. But when it comes to working in Fortran, you will find that writing out a code can be nice and simple and it won't take that long for you to learn it and start working on your own.

This guidebook is going to take some time to help you learn how to work with the Fortran code. We are going to start out with writing some of our own codes while learning about some of the basics that come with Fortran. We will then move on to working with strings and arrays, understanding how the loops work, and even working with conditional statements. These are actually really important parts of working with a coding language, but since Fortran is so simple to work with that you will be able to add them into a code in no time.

When you are ready to get started on writing some of your own codes and want to get into the world of coding, working with Fortran is one of the best options to help you to get this all done. It is an older language that is meant for beginners and you will be able to catch on to it in no time at all. Use this guidebook to learn what you need to know in order to get the Fortran language to work for you.

www.ingramcontent.com/pod-product-compliance
Lightning Source LLC
Chambersburg PA
CBHW070721210526
45170CB00021B/1393